AF230785

Little Fox's Hidden Disability

Written by Lisa McArthur-Collins
Illustrated by Maira Qaisar
Edited by Michelle Wanasundera

First Printing, 2026

Published Independently by Little Wings Publishing
and Lisa McArthur-Collins
www.littlewingspublishing.com
hello@littlewingspublishing.com

ISBN
978-1-7638789-6-9 Paperback
978-1-7638789-7-6 Hardcover
978-1-7638789-8-3 eBook

Little Fox's
Hidden Disability

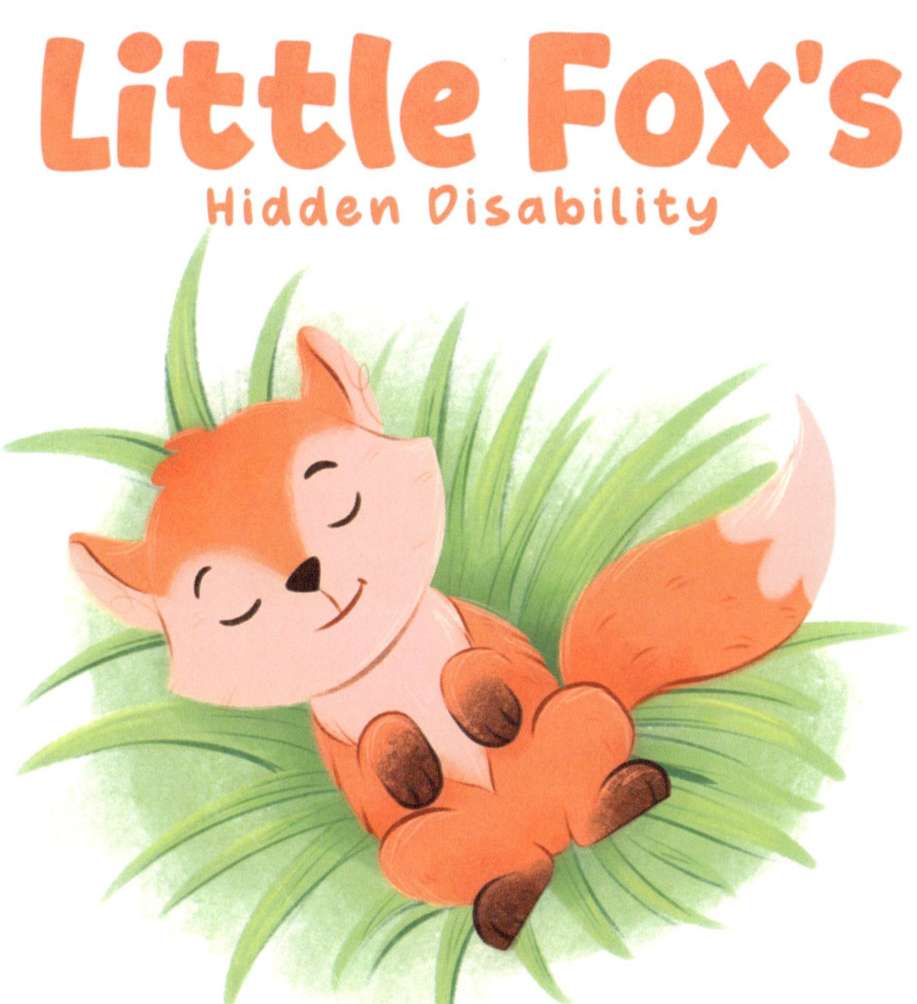

Written by Lisa McArthur-Collins
Illustrated by Maira Qaisar

It all started when we left the Spring Festival early.
I felt tired all over, from the tops of my ears to the tip
of my fluffy tail.

It all started when we lef
I felt tired all over, from
of m

"Why do I need to go home?"
I asked Mama.
"Why can't I stay for longer like my friends?"

"Because you find it more difficult than they do.
You have a hidden disability." Mama said.

"What's a hidden disa.." but before I could finish,
I was sound asleep in my bed.

The next day, I couldn't stop wondering...
What is my hidden disability?
And why is it hiding?

Is it shy, or afraid?

I look under my tail...

It's not there.

Behind my log...

Nope!

Maybe I'll ask Mama.

"I will tell you all about it later," she says.

But I can't wait until later...

PLIP! PLOP!

"It's a nice day for a swim, Turtle!
Have you seen my disability?" I ask.
"I can't find it anywhere."

Turtle blinks slowly.
"No, Little Fox. But check out my disability.
It's easy to spot; this crack here never quite healed."

I sigh. "I can't find mine anywhere.
It must be invisible…"

TWEET! TWEET!
"Oh, hi, Robin. I'm looking for my disability. Is it hiding in your nest?"
Robin shakes his feathers. "No, Little Fox. But see my glasses right here. They help my eyes see clearly."

I peek inside Robin's nest just in case,

but...

my disability is still not there!

CRUNCH!
CRUNCH!
Hmm, maybe Bunny has seen it!

"Nice wheels, Bunny!
I wonder, have you seen my disability?"

Bunny twitches her nose.

"No, Little Fox, but my legs don't work the same as yours, so I use my wheelchair to get around. That's my disability," Bunny smiles.
"Maybe yours doesn't want to be seen."

I look under my paws,

but...

it's still not there!

SCRATCH!
SCRATCH!

"That looks fun, Bear.
I want to know if you've seen
my disability?" I ask.

Bear cups a paw around his ear.

"No, Little Fox, but I wear this
to help me hear."

Little Fox looks closer and spots
a tiny hearing aid behind Bear's
fuzzy ear.

"It helps me listen to
the birds sing,"
says Bear proudly.

I listen too, but... it's still not there!

TAP! TAP!

"Deer, have you seen my
disability?" I ask.

Deer smiles.
"No, Little Fox. I don't see very well.
I use a cane to find my way."

Deer takes a careful step.
"I listen to the wind;
it helps guide my steps."

**I walk beside Deer for a while,
so we can find our way together.**

But my disability... it's still not there.

SPLISH! SPLASH!

I follow the sound and find Otter resting by the stream. I feel like resting too.

"I can't find my disability!" I cry.

Otter taps a small tablet. A clear voice says, "That's tough, Little Fox. I'm sorry I haven't seen it."

"Wow," I say.
"You talk with a tablet?"

Otter nods and presses another button.
The tablet says, "Yes."

I smile. "That's so cool."

I look around for my disability,
but...
it's still not there!

I plop onto the grass with a sigh.
I've looked everywhere!
If it's hidden, how will I know what it is,
and how will anyone know it's real?

Suddenly, the forest feels very busy.
Everyone is heading home to their hollows, logs, and nests.

**SWOOSH!
SCREECH!
SCAMPER!
STOMP!**

A gentle breeze brushes my fur.
I can't see it... but I can feel it all around me.

I realise my disability feels a lot like the wind.

I'm exhausted after my day of searching!

"Still looking for your hidden disability?" Mama asks.

I nod. "I can't find it anywhere."

"That's because yours hides inside,
Little Fox," says Mama.
"It's part of how your body and brain work.
You can't see it, but it's always with you."

"Like the wind?" I whisper.

Mama smiles.
"Very much like the wind."

"But it's not the wind, so what is it?"
I ask.

"Some disabilities make it hard to move, speak,
listen, or stay calm," says Mama Fox.

"Yours means your brain feels things very strongly. That's why noise and crowds can be too much sometimes."

I think about that.

"So it's not bad or missing, it's just different?"

Mama Fox smiles and pulls me close.

**"Different and wonderful. But because it's hidden,
some people don't know it's there.
There are ways to help others understand, too.
Like sharing your story, or wearing this."**

**In Mama Fox's paw is a
small sunflower.**

"This little sunflower tells people you might need a bit of extra kindness and some space when things get a little loud or busy."

The next day, I wear my sunflower proudly.
It doesn't make my hidden disability appear,
but it helps others see me a little better.

My friends notice it right away.

Turtle, Robin, Bunny, Bear, Deer,
and Otter all smile.

"Take your time, Little Fox," they say.

Now I know my disability was never
really lost.

It's a part of me,
and I don't need to find it anymore.

And for the first time, I don't feel that any part of me is hidden at all.

And it feels so good to be me, from the tops of my ears to the tip of my fluffy tail!

Little Wings Publishing is proud to support the Hidden Disability Sunflower.
A portion of sales from this book helps provide free sunflower lanyards to those who need them.

Hidden disabilities are conditions that aren't always visible, like autism, ADHD, sensory processing challenges, anxiety, or chronic illness.

They may affect how someone moves, feels, learns, or communicates.

The sunflower symbol is a subtle way for people to show they may need extra patience, time, or understanding.

Not all disabilities can be seen, but all deserve kindness.

To learn more, visit the Hidden Disabilities Sunflower website:
www.hdsunflower.com

If you see someone wearing a sunflower lanyard or pin, they may need a little extra patience, time, or understanding.

Why a Sunflower?
The Sunflower reflects the idea of confidence, growth and strength shown by people with non-visible disabilities, as well as introducing happiness and positivity